The Tower of Babel

Rob Waring

Series Editor Rob Waring

Level 1 - ❸

The Tower of Babel

Rob Waring

© 2017 Seed Learning, Inc.

Series Editor: Rob Waring
Acquisitions Editor: Liana Robinson
Copy Editor: Casey Malarcher
Cover/Interior Design: Andy Roh

ISBN: 978-1-9464-5202-3

10 9 8 7 6 5 4 3 2 1
21 20 19 18 17

Contents

Our Languages 4

The Great Flood 7

The Building Begins 9

An Unhappy God 11

Many Versions 14

How True Is This Story? 15

So What Do You Think? 17

Comprehension Questions 18

Glossary 19

World History Timeline 21

Our Languages

The world is full of languages. There are more than 5,000 languages in use today.

There are thousands of ways to say a simple word like "Hello."

Some of the world's languages

Listening to a language

Ways to say, "Hello!"

Many cultures together

Mixed races, mixed languages

Many of the world's languages are related. French, Italian, and Spanish are Latin languages. They share many words and some grammar. German, Swedish, and English are related, too.

Where did all these languages come from?

An old pen and
some papers

There are many stories about where our languages came from. Many of these stories are similar to the story of the Tower of Babel.

To understand this story, we must begin with the flood.

Egyptian writing on a wall

The Great Flood

Long ago, there was a great flood. The world was covered with water. Noah and his family were safe on his ark.

Noah's ark during the flood

After the water had gone away, the only people left on earth were Noah and his family. They spoke one language.

A flood

The historic city of Babylon

Some of Noah's children's children went east to a land called Shinar, sometimes said to be Babylon, in modern-day Iraq.

Some years later, these people decided to build a tower "tall enough to reach heaven."

They wanted to be one people, close to God.

Tower of Babel (Babylon), a famous painting by Pieter Brueghel the Elder created in 1563

The Building Begins

They spent a long time building the tall tower. Thousands of people worked long and hard every day.

They made the bricks with mud from the earth and dried them in the hot sun.

Clay bricks drying in the sun

Women making mud bricks in India

Mixing mud to make bricks

The tower got bigger and bigger, taller and taller, and the people were happy. They were working together as one people.

Walls made with mud bricks

A painting by Tissot of the building of the tower

A brick tower in Narin Qal'eh, Iran

An Unhappy God

The story says that one day, God came down to see this tower. He was not happy. He did not like the tower. It did not honor Him. The people wanted to make themselves as great as God.

The Tower of Babel by Hans Bol

Light from the sky

God made the people speak in different languages, so they could no longer be one people.

He wanted to make them feel bad for building such a tower.

Wieża Babel – A Polish picture of God sending people away

People going in different directions

The people were confused and went to all corners of the world. They took their new languages with them.

The Confusion of Tongues

Leaving for a new land

13

Many Versions

A different version of the story says Nimrod, their leader, wanted power for himself. He did not want the people to think of God, but think of him. So he ordered the people to make the tower for him.

Nimrod's fortress

This version of the story says God was angry that the people were building the tower for Nimrod and not God.

Nimrod's people building the tower

How True Is This Story?

Historians have found some of the places mentioned in the many versions of the Tower of Babel, although no one has found the tower.

The Tower of Babel
by Tobias Verhaecht, 1600

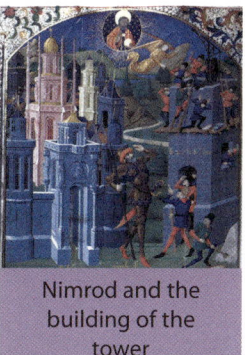

Nimrod and the building of the tower

A Russian version of the story

The Great Flood by Jan Nagel (1560-1602)

Tower of Babel story in cuneiform

There is doubt that people thousands of years ago could build such a tall tower with ancient tools and techniques.

Some scientists say there is no evidence of a great flood, so how can there have been only one language?

But maybe scientists just need more time. We are not completely sure how the pyramids were built, yet we can see them. And evidence of the flood would be deep under the ocean—making it hard to find.

So What Do You Think?

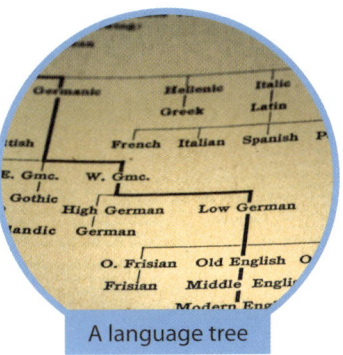

Most modern researchers say many languages developed independently all over the world. They mixed and changed over time to create new languages. These became the languages we know today.

A language tree

Where do you think the world's languages come from?

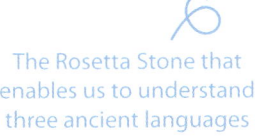

The Rosetta Stone that enables us to understand three ancient languages

Comprehension Questions

1. There are … languages in the world.
   (a) only a few
   (b) hundreds of
   (c) thousands of
   (d) millions of

2. French and Italian are both… languages.
   (a) English
   (b) Latin
   (c) German
   (d) Babel's

3. We say German and English are…
   (a) relations.
   (b) relative.
   (c) relatively.
   (d) related.

4. In the Great Flood, what covered the earth?
   (a) People
   (b) Noah
   (c) Language
   (d) Water

5. The people on Noah's Ark…
   (a) were wet.
   (b) were hungry.
   (c) spoke one language.
   (d) made mud.

6. In one version, Nimrod told the people to…
   (a) build a tower.
   (b) take Noah's Ark.
   (c) stop the flood.
   (d) go to heaven.

7. They made the tower…
   (a) with bricks.
   (b) together.
   (c) taller and taller.
   (d) All of the above

8. God…
   (a) told the people to build faster.
   (b) gave them all different languages.
   (c) sent a second flood.
   (d) All of the above

9. Many people say this story is…
   (a) not true.
   (b) funny.
   (c) full of evidence.
   (d) sad.

10. Many scientists believe that our languages…
    (a) have always been mixed.
    (b) are dying.
    (c) are modern.
    (d) are creative.

Glossary

- **ancient** very old

- **brick** a hard block of mud used for building

- **confused** not knowing why, or how, something happened

- **enable** to allow us to do something

- **evidence** facts that are true about something

- **flood** a large amount of water covering an area of land

- **historian** a person who studies history

- **modern** concerning this time period; nowadays

- **mud** wet earth or soil

- **related** to be connected in some way

- **researcher** a scientist who studies things carefully

- **technique** a method or way to do something

- **tower** a very tall, thin building

- **version** a story or description that is different in some way from another person's story or description

Image Credit/Pages

World History Timeline

This chart shows a rough overview of world history.
Some of the dates have been simplified.

World History Timeline

2900 BC	2800 BC	2700 BC	2600 BC	2500 BC

Pyramids of Giza
(built c. 2550-2490 BC)

Narmer, Egyptian King
(c. 3000 BC)

Cuneiform (c. 3000 BC-100 AD)

Old Egyptian Kingdom (c. 2686 BC)

2900 BC	2800 BC	2700 BC	2600 BC	2500 BC

◄ 5000 BC   Mesopotamia (Sumerians)

◄ 3100 BC   Early Dynastic Period of Egypt   Old Egyptian Kingdom

◄ 3650 BC   Minoan Civilization (Crete)

Early Bronze Age

2900 BC	2800 BC	2700 BC	2600 BC	2500 BC

World History Timeline

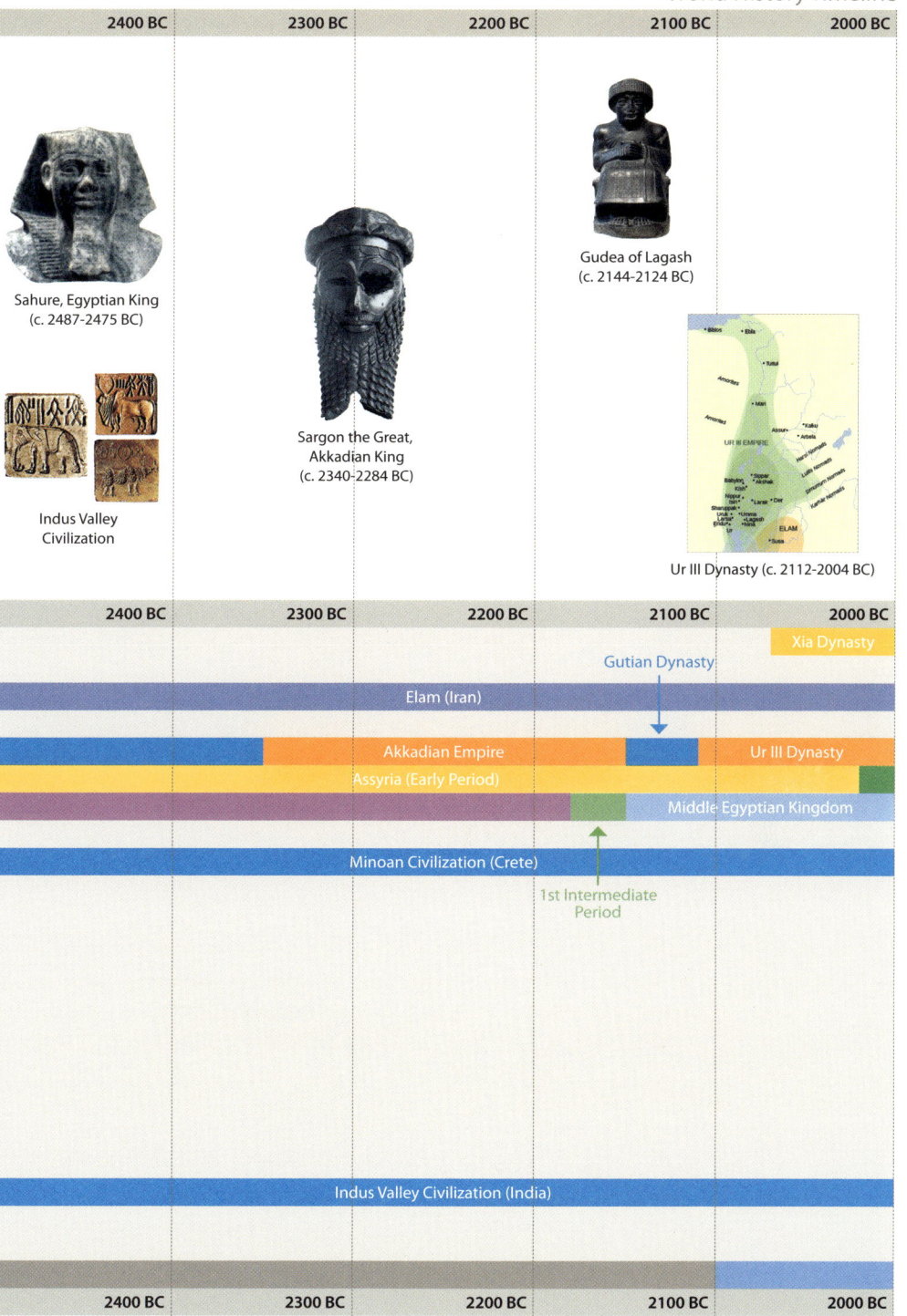

2400 BC	2300 BC	2200 BC	2100 BC	2000 BC

Sahure, Egyptian King
(c. 2487-2475 BC)

Indus Valley
Civilization

Sargon the Great,
Akkadian King
(c. 2340-2284 BC)

Gudea of Lagash
(c. 2144-2124 BC)

Ur III Dynasty (c. 2112-2004 BC)

2400 BC	2300 BC	2200 BC	2100 BC	2000 BC

Xia Dynasty

Gutian Dynasty

Elam (Iran)

Akkadian Empire

Ur III Dynasty

Assyria (Early Period)

Middle Egyptian Kingdom

Minoan Civilization (Crete)

1st Intermediate
Period

Indus Valley Civilization (India)

2400 BC	2300 BC	2200 BC	2100 BC	2000 BC

World History Timeline

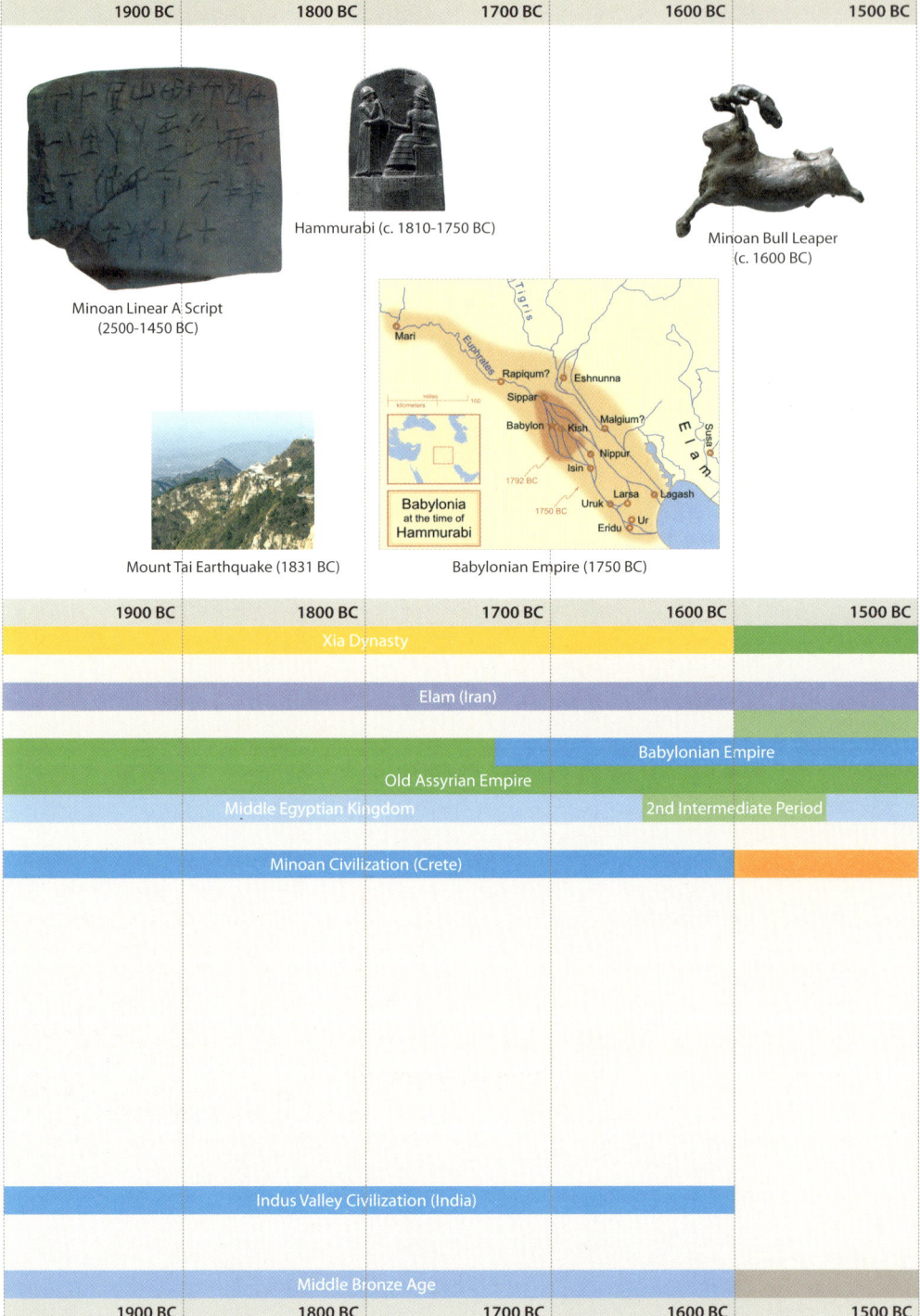

1900 BC	1800 BC	1700 BC	1600 BC	1500 BC

Minoan Linear A Script
(2500-1450 BC)

Hammurabi (c. 1810-1750 BC)

Minoan Bull Leaper
(c. 1600 BC)

Mount Tai Earthquake (1831 BC)

Babylonia
at the time of
Hammurabi

Babylonian Empire (1750 BC)

1900 BC	1800 BC	1700 BC	1600 BC	1500 BC

Xia Dynasty

Elam (Iran)

Babylonian Empire

Old Assyrian Empire

Middle Egyptian Kingdom

2nd Intermediate Period

Minoan Civilization (Crete)

Indus Valley Civilization (India)

Middle Bronze Age

1900 BC	1800 BC	1700 BC	1600 BC	1500 BC

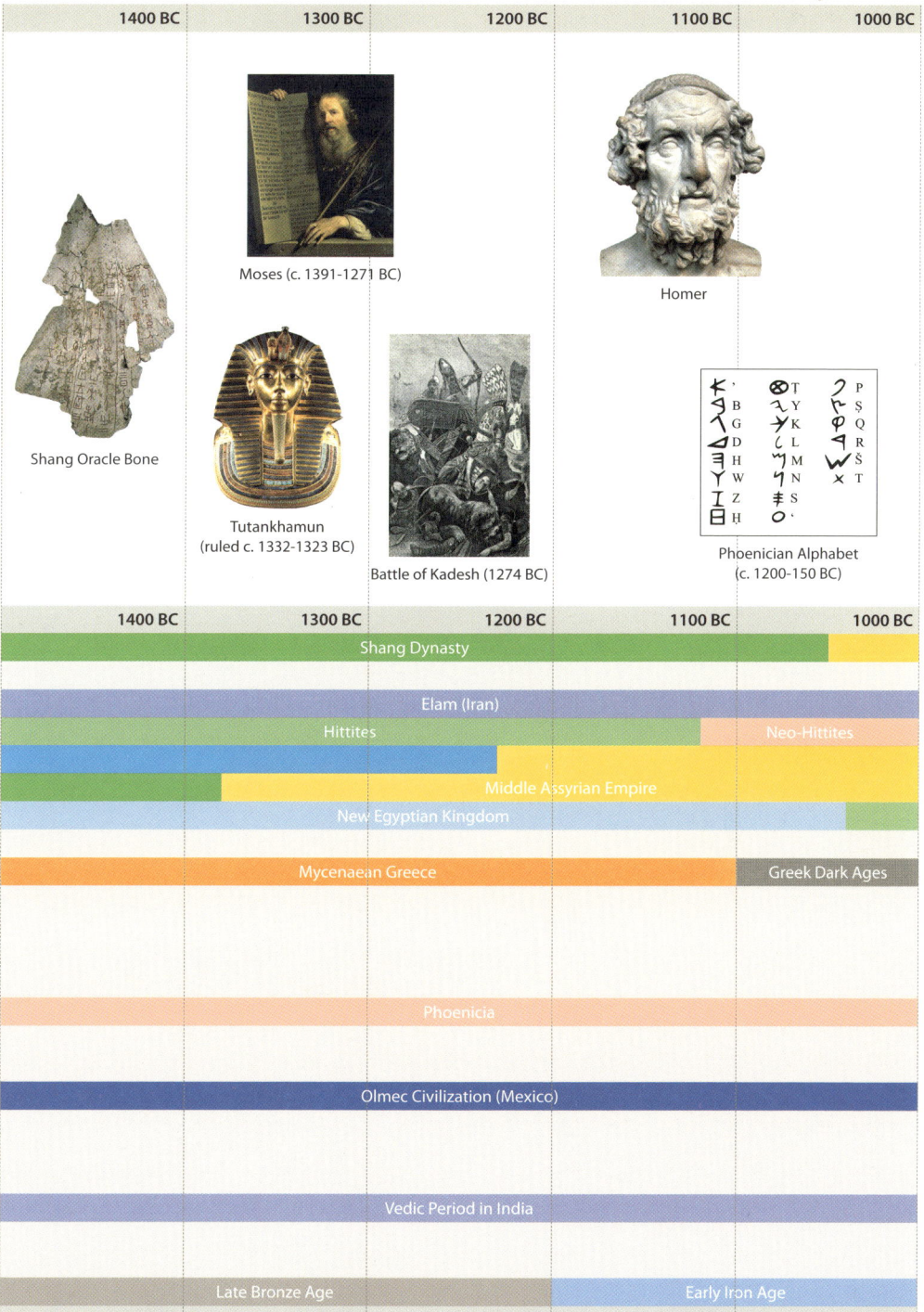

1400 BC	1300 BC	1200 BC	1100 BC	1000 BC

Moses (c. 1391-1271 BC)

Homer

Shang Oracle Bone

Tutankhamun
(ruled c. 1332-1323 BC)

Battle of Kadesh (1274 BC)

Phoenician Alphabet
(c. 1200-150 BC)

1400 BC	1300 BC	1200 BC	1100 BC	1000 BC

Shang Dynasty

Elam (Iran)

Hittites

Neo-Hittites

Middle Assyrian Empire

New Egyptian Kingdom

Mycenaean Greece

Greek Dark Ages

Phoenicia

Olmec Civilization (Mexico)

Vedic Period in India

Late Bronze Age

Early Iron Age

1400 BC	1300 BC	1200 BC	1100 BC	1000 BC

World History Timeline

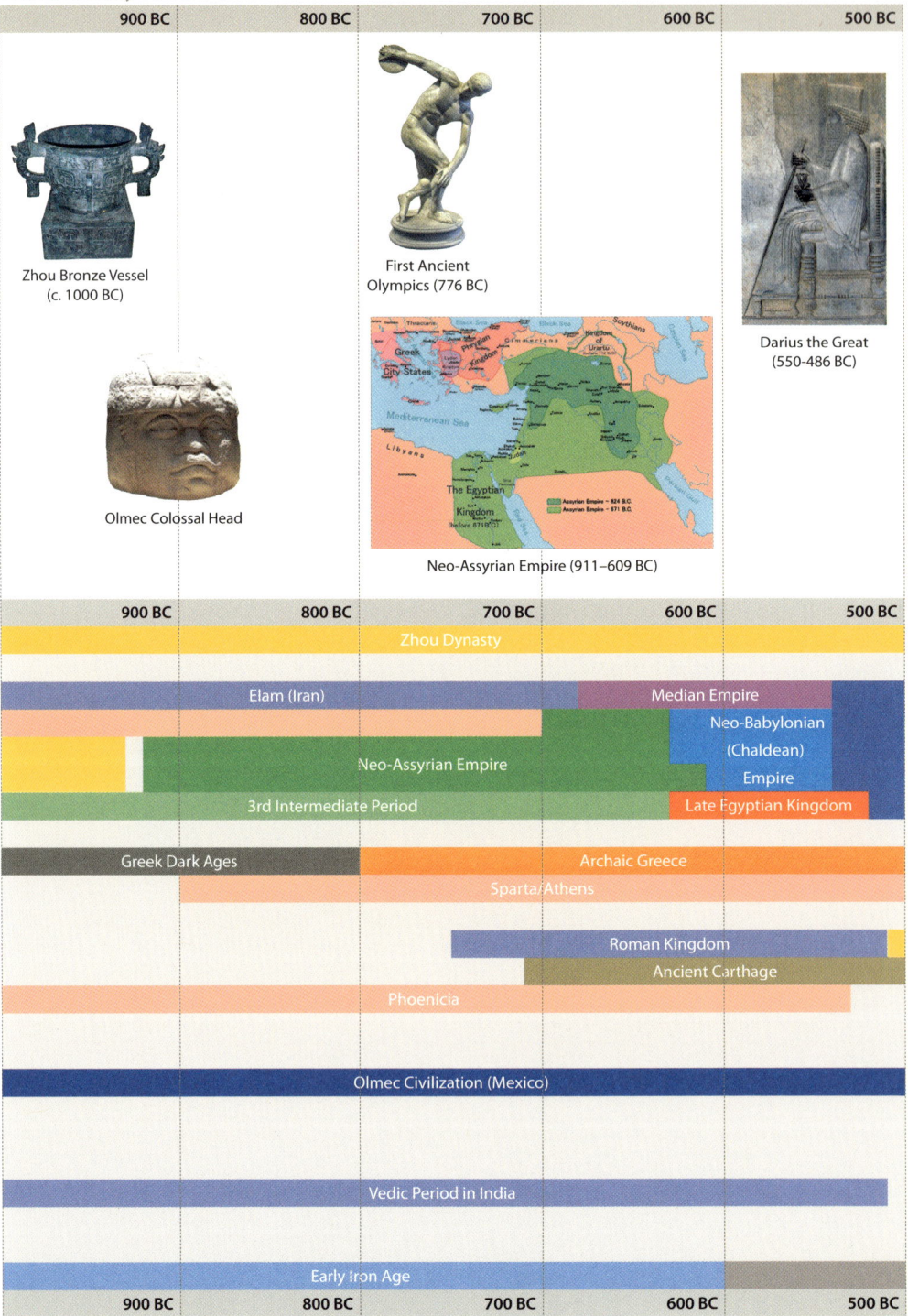

900 BC	800 BC	700 BC	600 BC	500 BC

Zhou Bronze Vessel
(c. 1000 BC)

First Ancient
Olympics (776 BC)

Darius the Great
(550-486 BC)

Olmec Colossal Head

Neo-Assyrian Empire (911–609 BC)

900 BC	800 BC	700 BC	600 BC	500 BC

Zhou Dynasty

Elam (Iran)

Median Empire

Neo-Babylonian (Chaldean) Empire

Neo-Assyrian Empire

3rd Intermediate Period

Late Egyptian Kingdom

Greek Dark Ages

Archaic Greece

Sparta/Athens

Roman Kingdom

Ancient Carthage

Phoenicia

Olmec Civilization (Mexico)

Vedic Period in India

Early Iron Age

900 BC	800 BC	700 BC	600 BC	500 BC

400 BC	300 BC	200 BC	100 BC	0

Alexander the Great
(356-323 BC)

Julius Caesar
(100-44 BC)

Cleopatra
(69-30 BC)

Hannibal
(247-183 BC)

Battle of Salamis
(480 BC)

Seleucid Empire (312-63 BC)

Rossetta Stone
(created 196 BC)

400 BC	300 BC	200 BC	100 BC	0

Zhou Dynasty

Qin

Han Dynasty

Achaemenid (Persian) Empire

Alexander the Great

Parthian Empire

Seleucid Empire
Ptolemaic Kingdom
(Hellenistic Greece)

Classical Greece

Sparta/Athens

Roman Empire

Roman Republic

Roman Empire

Maurya Empire

Middle Iron Age

400 BC	300 BC	200 BC	100 BC	0

World History Timeline

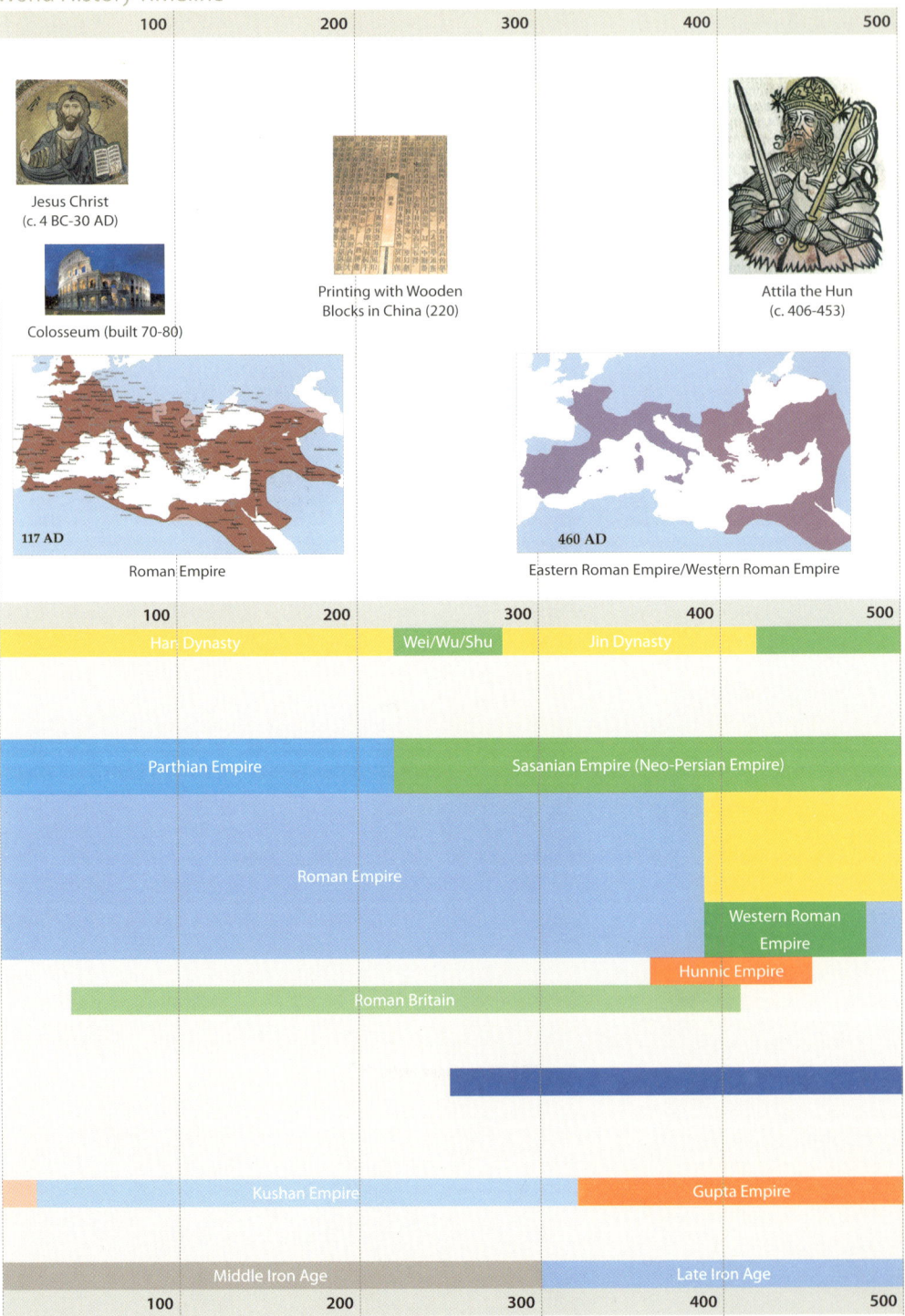

| | 100 | 200 | 300 | 400 | 500 |

Jesus Christ
(c. 4 BC-30 AD)

Colosseum (built 70-80)

Printing with Wooden
Blocks in China (220)

Attila the Hun
(c. 406-453)

117 AD

Roman Empire

460 AD

Eastern Roman Empire/Western Roman Empire

| | 100 | 200 | 300 | 400 | 500 |

Han Dynasty

Wei/Wu/Shu

Jin Dynasty

Parthian Empire

Sasanian Empire (Neo-Persian Empire)

Roman Empire

Western Roman Empire

Hunnic Empire

Roman Britain

Kushan Empire

Gupta Empire

Middle Iron Age

Late Iron Age

| | 100 | 200 | 300 | 400 | 500 |

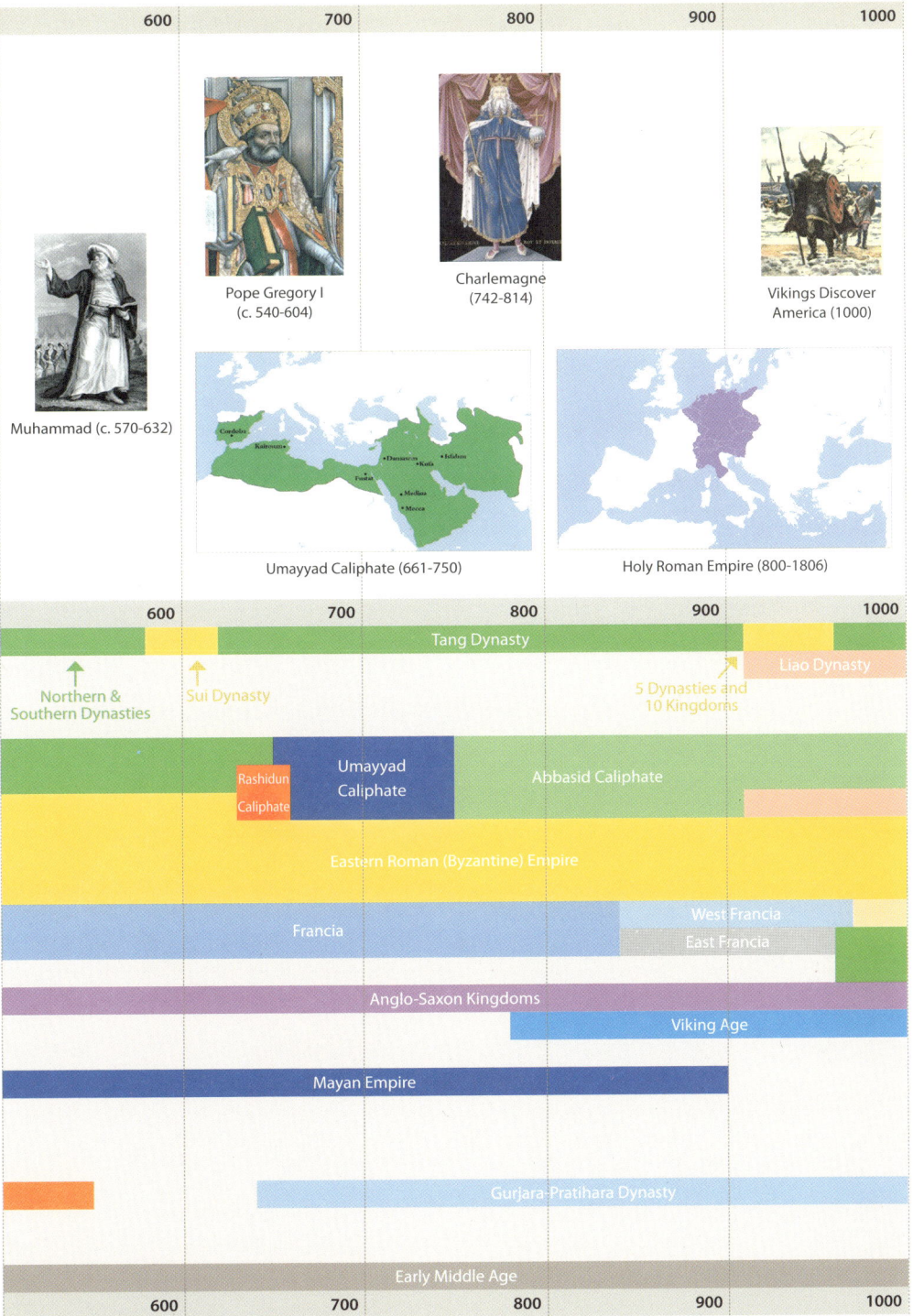

Pope Gregory I
(c. 540-604)

Charlemagne
(742-814)

Vikings Discover
America (1000)

Muhammad (c. 570-632)

Umayyad Caliphate (661-750)

Holy Roman Empire (800-1806)

| | 600 | 700 | 800 | 900 | 1000 |

Tang Dynasty

Liao Dynasty

Northern &
Southern Dynasties

Sui Dynasty

5 Dynasties and
10 Kingdoms

Rashidun
Caliphate

Umayyad
Caliphate

Abbasid Caliphate

Eastern Roman (Byzantine) Empire

Francia

West Francia

East Francia

Anglo-Saxon Kingdoms

Viking Age

Mayan Empire

Gurjara-Pratihara Dynasty

Early Middle Age

| | 600 | 700 | 800 | 900 | 1000 |

World History Timeline

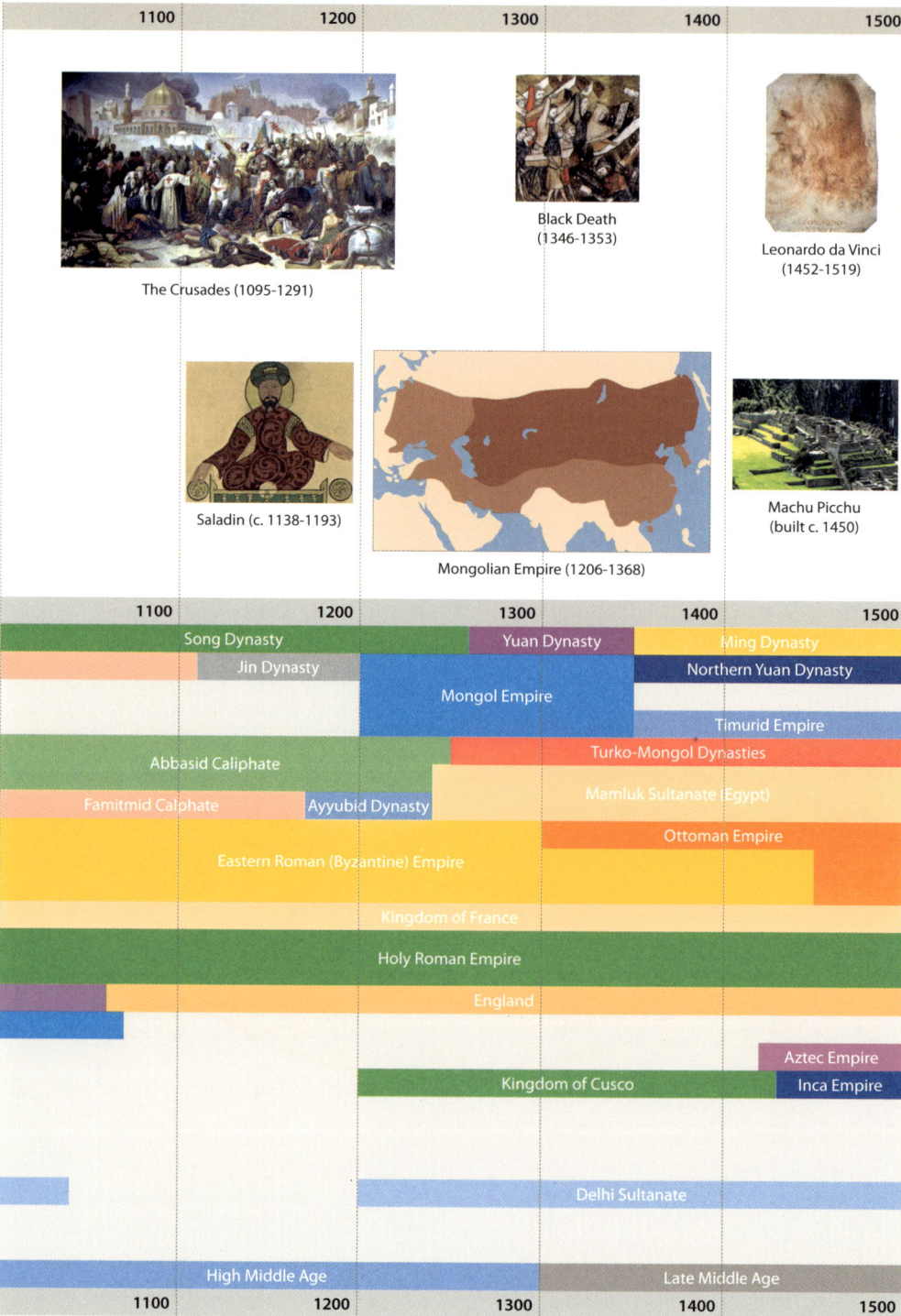

The Crusades (1095-1291)

Black Death (1346-1353)

Leonardo da Vinci (1452-1519)

Saladin (c. 1138-1193)

Mongolian Empire (1206-1368)

Machu Picchu (built c. 1450)

	1100	1200	1300	1400	1500

- Song Dynasty
- Yuan Dynasty
- Ming Dynasty
- Jin Dynasty
- Northern Yuan Dynasty
- Mongol Empire
- Timurid Empire
- Abbasid Caliphate
- Turko-Mongol Dynasties
- Famitmid Calphate
- Ayyubid Dynasty
- Mamluk Sultanate (Egypt)
- Ottoman Empire
- Eastern Roman (Byzantine) Empire
- Kingdom of France
- Holy Roman Empire
- England
- Aztec Empire
- Kingdom of Cusco
- Inca Empire
- Delhi Sultanate
- High Middle Age
- Late Middle Age

1100	1200	1300	1400	1500